Workouts for the Intermediate Cellist

by Cassia Harvey

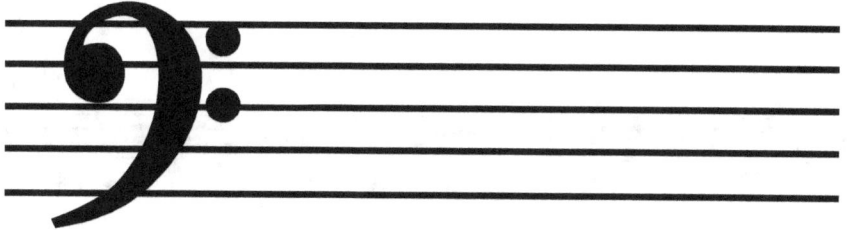

CHP190

©2007 by C. Harvey Publications All Rights Reserved.

www.charveypublications.com - print books
www.learnstrings.com - PDF downloadable books
www.harveystringarrangements.com - chamber music

C string

Workouts for the Intermediate Cellist

Cassia Harvey

I = A String   II = D String
III = G String   IV = C String

Play this entire page on the C string.

©2007 C. Harvey Publications All Rights Reserved.

Play this entire page on the C string.

Play this entire page on the C string.

Workouts for the Intermediate Cellist ©2007 C. Harvey Publications All Rights Reserved.

Play this entire page on the C string.

G string

Play this entire page on the G string.

Play this entire page on the G string.

8

Play this entire page on the G string.

Workouts for the Intermediate Cellist

©2007 C. Harvey Publications All Rights Reserved.

Play this entire page on the G string.

D string

Play this entire page on the D string.

Workouts for the Intermediate Cellist

Play this entire page on the D string.

Play this entire page on the D string.

Workouts for the Intermediate Cellist ©2007 C. Harvey Publications All Rights Reserved.

Play this entire page on the D string.

A string

Workouts for the Intermediate Cellist

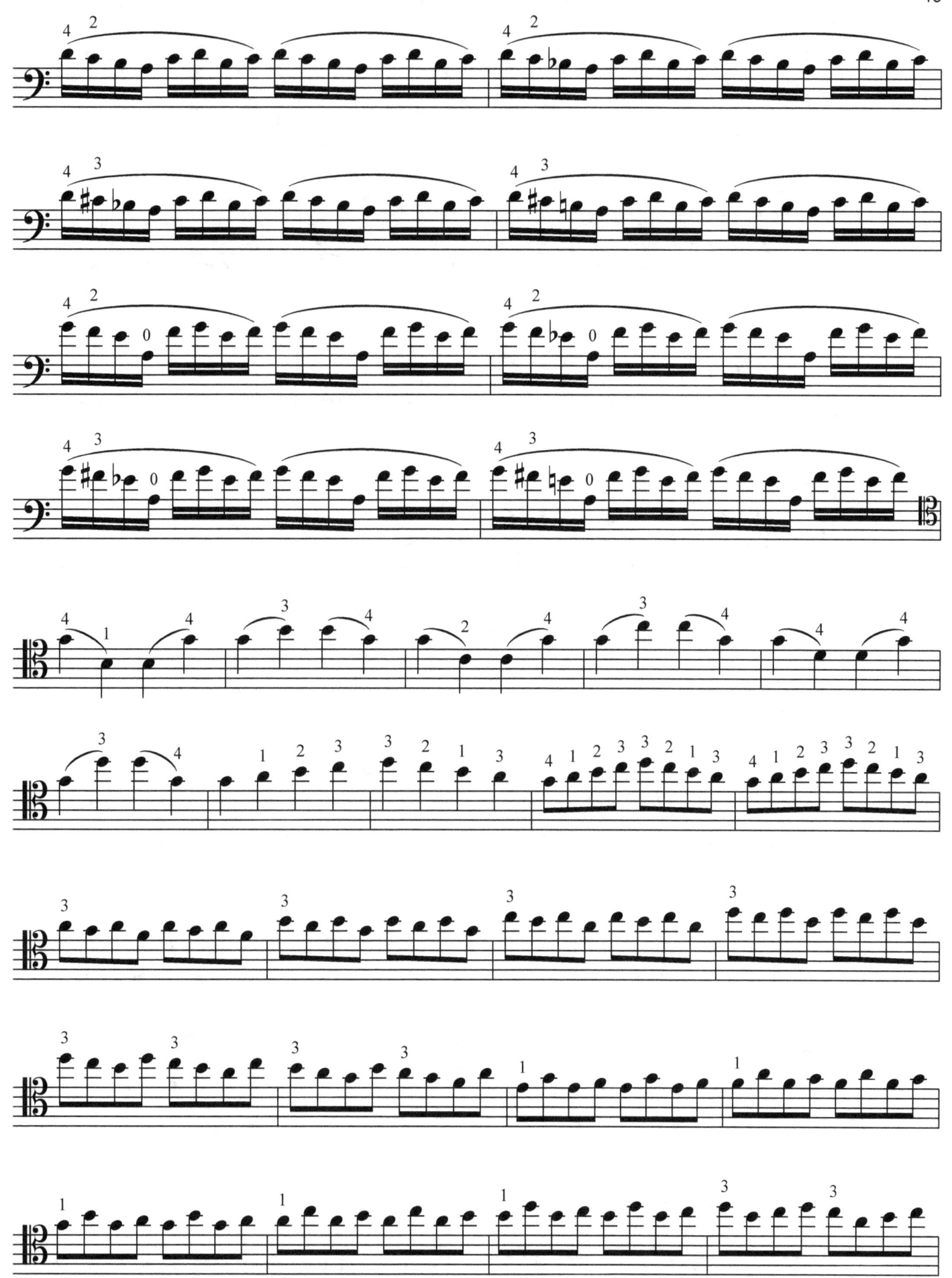

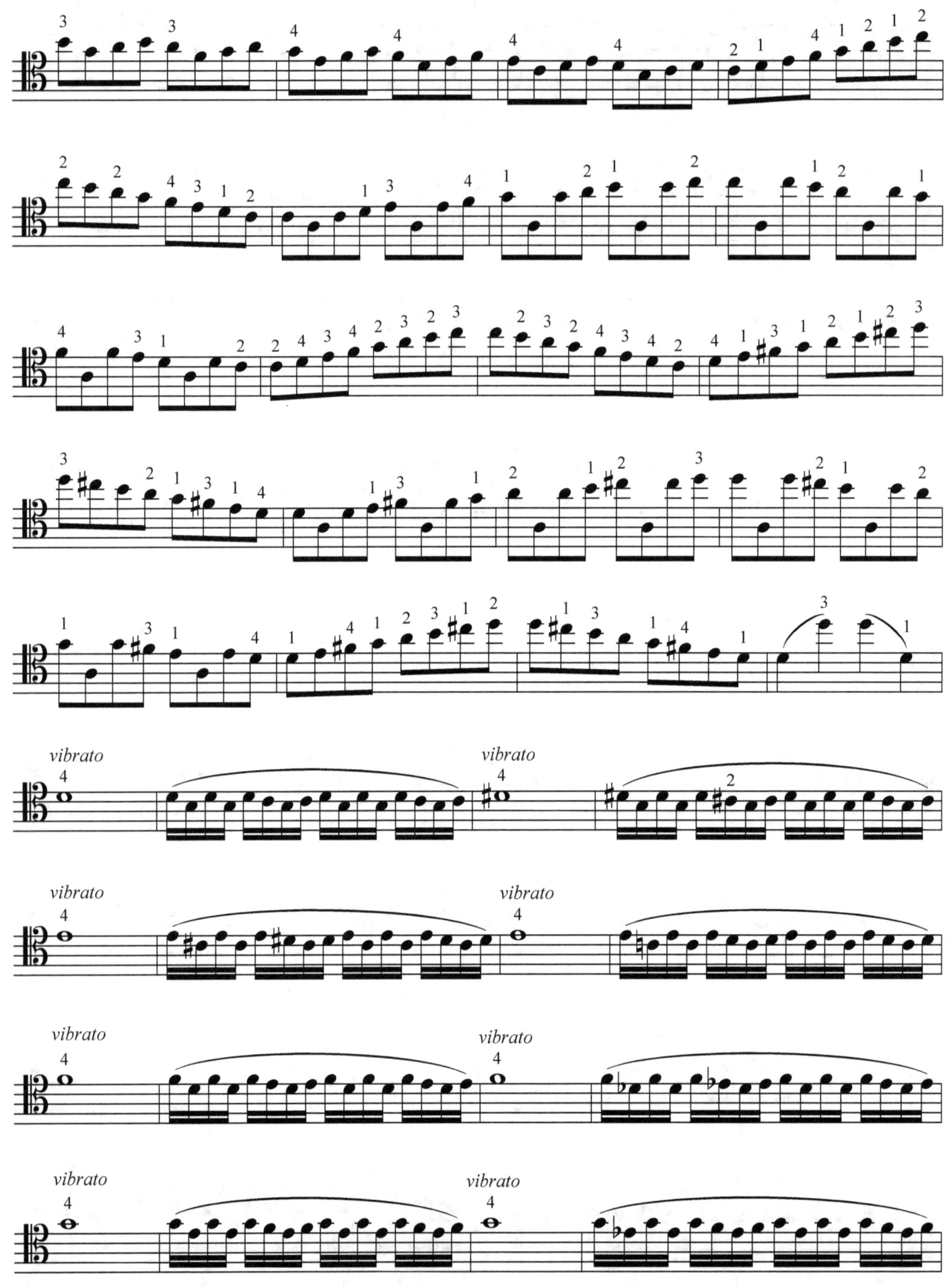

Across strings 1

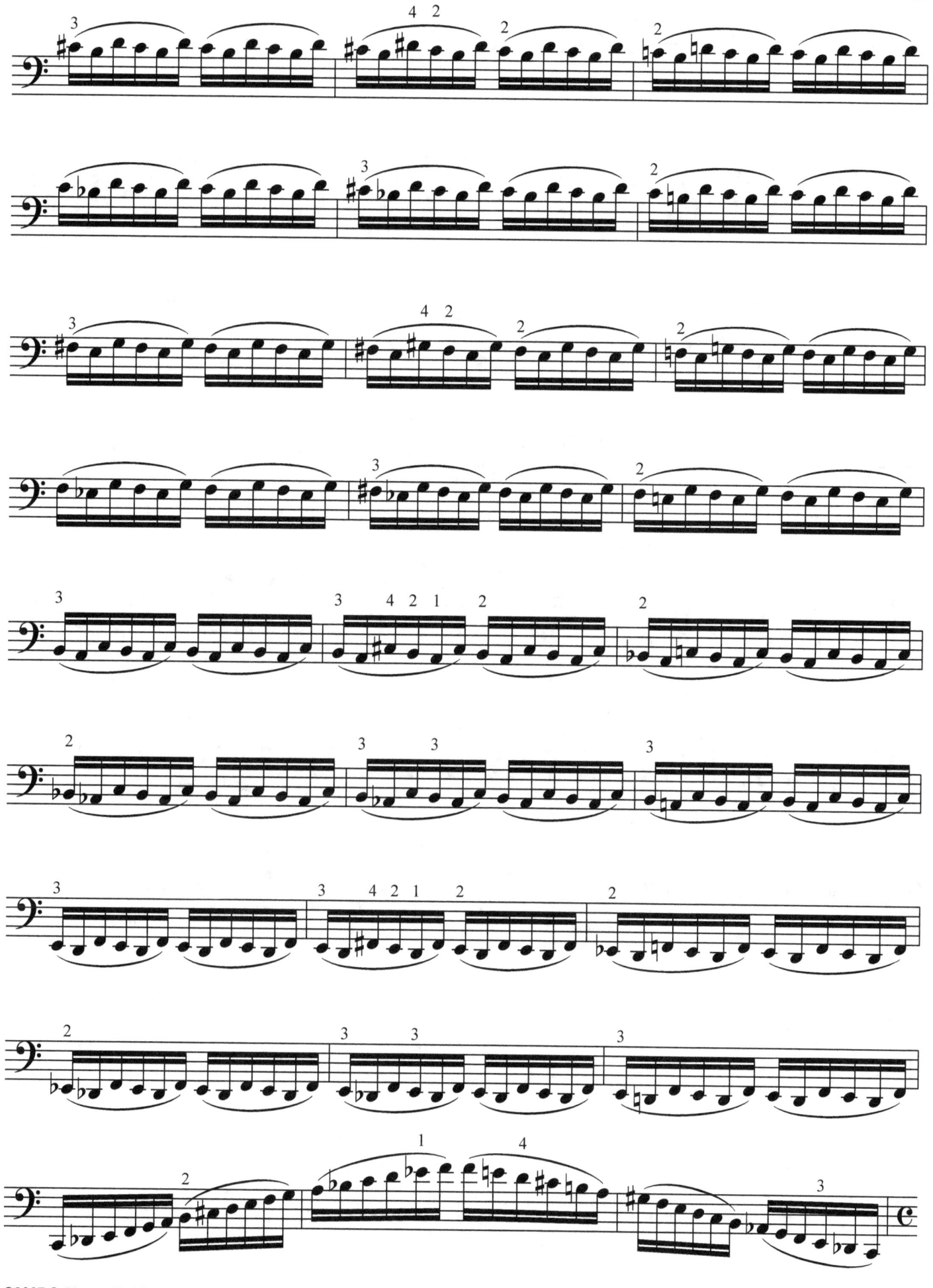

Across strings 2: Scales

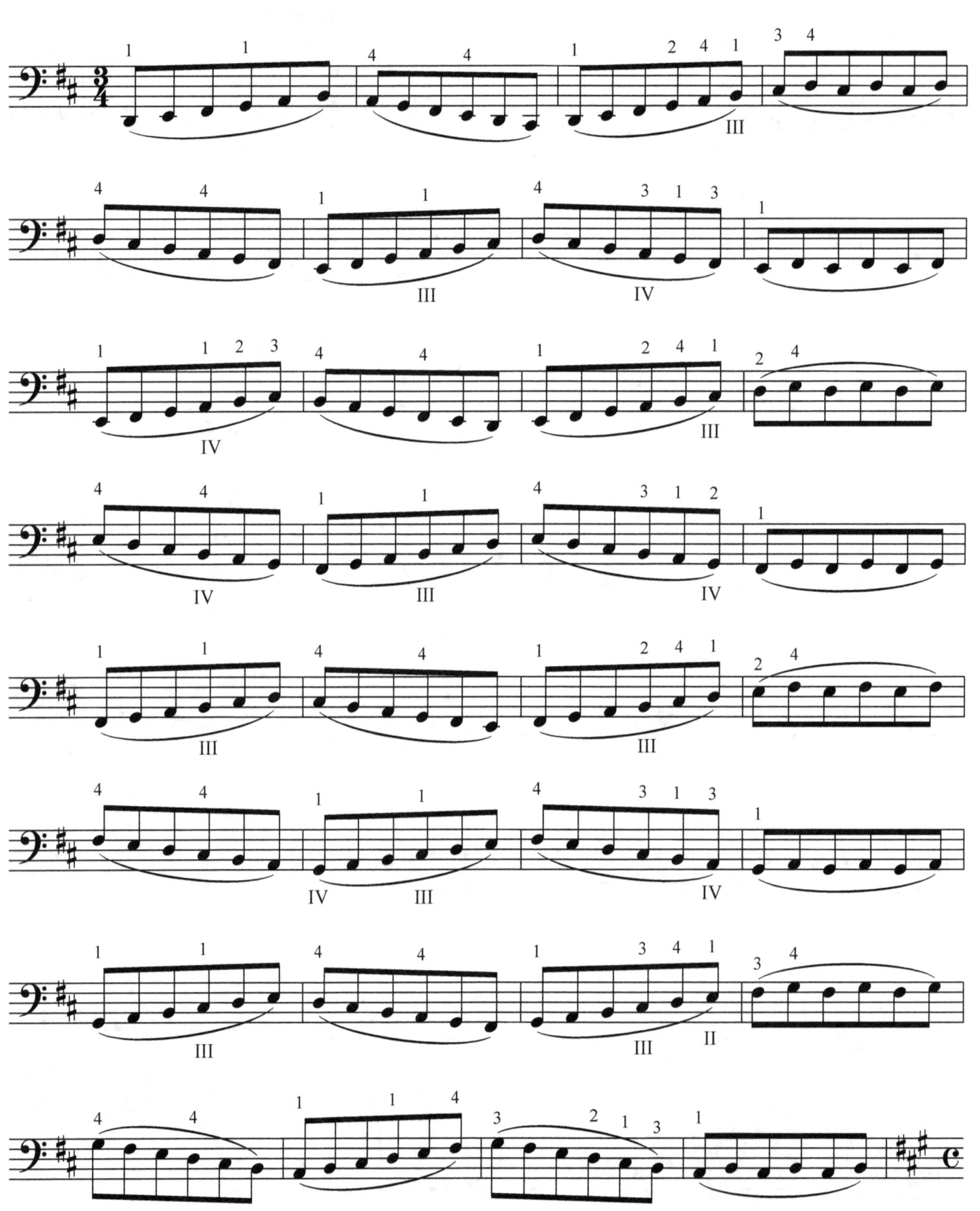

Workouts for the Intermediate Cellist

©2007 C. Harvey Publications All Rights Reserved.

Workouts for the Intermediate Cellist

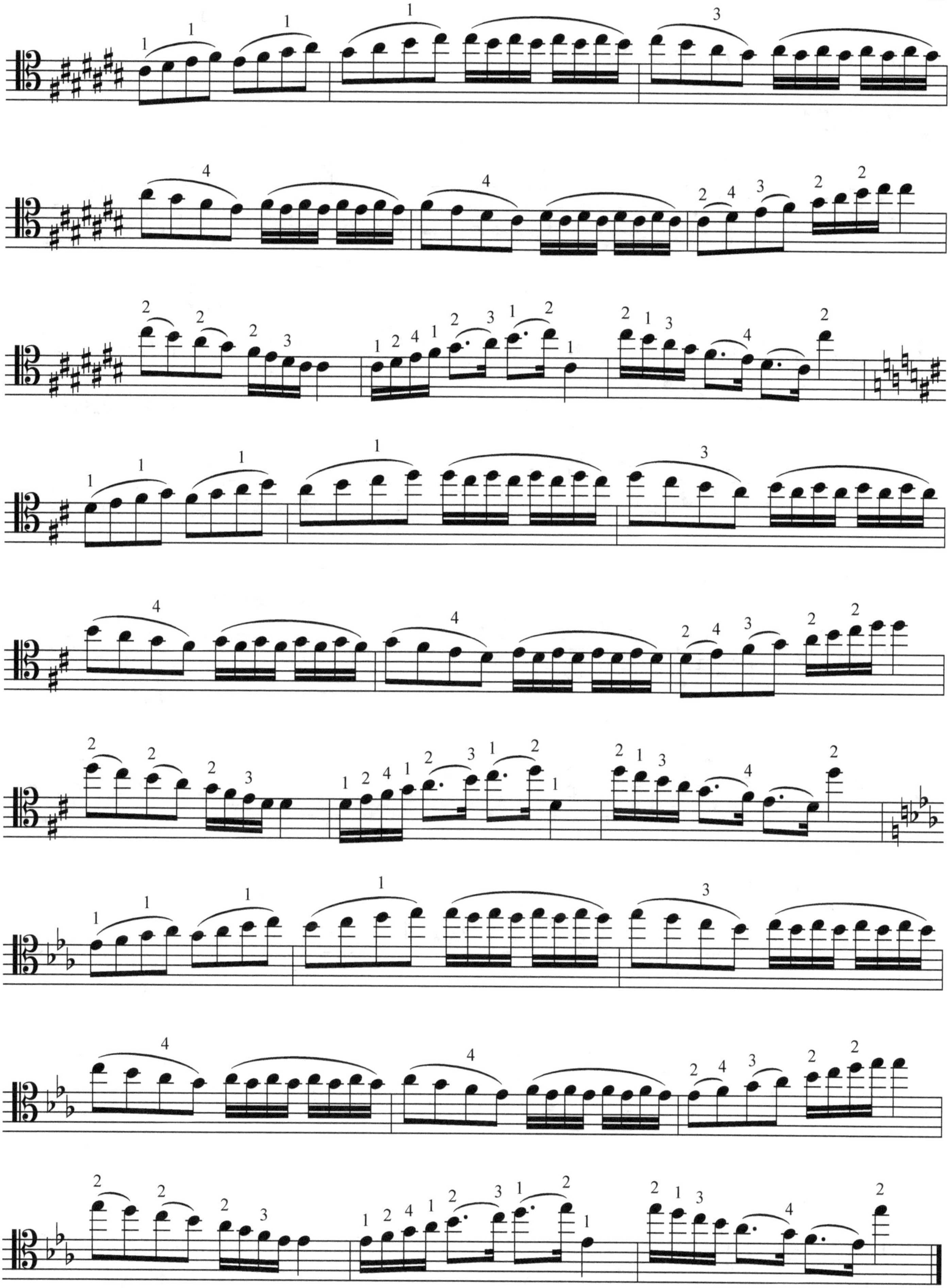

25

Across strings 3: Arpeggios

As you play this, change strings where it seems appropriate.

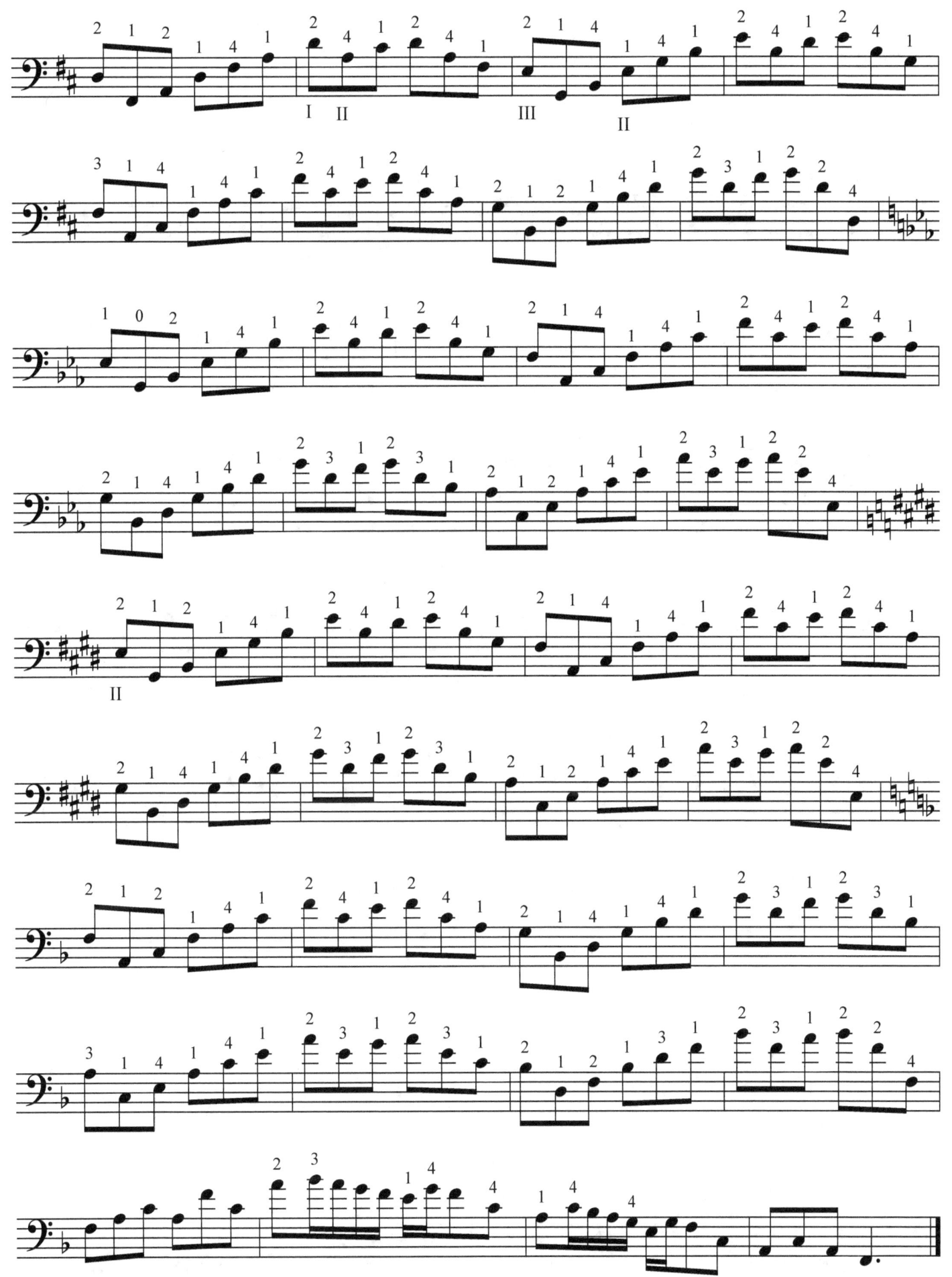

Across strings 4

Workouts for the Intermediate Cellist

©2007 C. Harvey Publications All Rights Reserved.

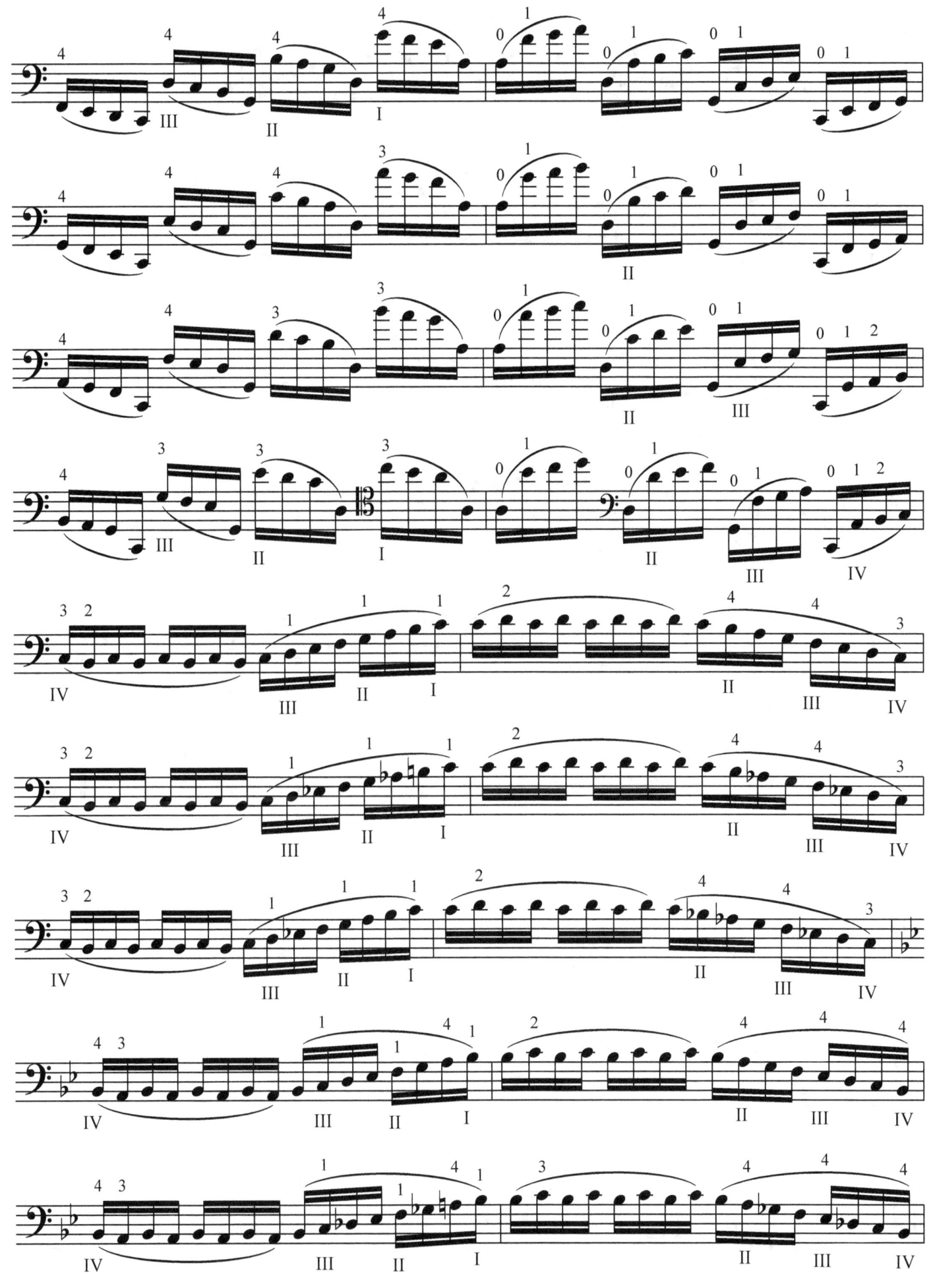

available from www.charveypublications.com: CHP244
Shifting in Keys for Cello, Book One
C Major Study No. 1

©2014 C. Harvey Publications All Rights Reserved.

www.ingramcontent.com/pod-product-compliance
Lightning Source LLC
Chambersburg PA
CBHW051429070526
44584CB00023B/3648